a winter of crows

Poems

by

Leticia A. Williams

Cover design by Gary Griffin, Jr. and Leticia Williams
Book design by Leticia A. Williams

Printed in the United States of America

First Printing: December 12, 2008-- ISBN 978-0-578-01675-7

For Mia and Christine

∞∞∞

Time forgets where we put things until even the thing itself has forgotten its name. But a person's spirit hunkers down in our minds and hearts and dwells there for as long as we can remember.

I dedicate this book to Christine M. Taaffe, who loved my words and encouraged me; and my beloved sister Charmian Varietta Williams, who gave me endless unconditional love and continues to serve as a forceful source of inspiration.

It is for them that I bind these words in an offering of remembrance and healing.

Namaste.

a winter of crows

ꝏꝏꝏ

I.

II.

III.

I.

Modern Times

I slip into the silence of things most simply
Pick over the bones of the charred bodies of change, in the gully of
this beautiful beast.

I count the wilting fruit of dead tomato plants and hack into the
neighbor's wireless connection.

I imagine these pirated waves as dipping into a
Pool of what other people owe me.

I throw my coins in to make good.

Autumn Day

Where, little one, have you gone
-with your bows and ribbons twisted
Through braids and ponytails
The sweet density of ice cream drops drying
On the skin, like lambs-wool, between your fingers?

Slips of grass hugging your pants
Daylight swooping down through tree-branches
To fasten its rays upon your mocha face.
Where, little brown girl, in this sunlit autumn paradise?

Your ghostly giggles trick me into false light
These are shadows, chasing echoes
With flight, like butterflies
Fluttering between the breezes
Our day had begun a fairy-tale.

Where, child, are your sugar-kissed lips now?

Winter

We know what winter tastes like
Of tin and earth
Of cold and water.

The smell in the wind before first snow
Breath light and lofting onto dense air.

The chill dwells in our bones
Like the frozen ground cleaves to the core.

The arctic nip of the bitter winds
Whipping us to leave it behind.

R & 13th (D.C., 2003)

Here all burnt and hollowed – Red Brick City,
Of these broken brick houses in a row, where Jean Toomer
Read and ate and slept.

Duke and Lena and Satchmo, all in spirit, between R and 13th
Streets.

Black fixtures all, and the remnants boarded up or demolished.
And mostly forgotten by all but an old black cabbie, who says even
he has forgotten some things his father and Granddaddy told him.

Much is lost here, like memories.
Everyday much is gained, but not the same.
Not worse, but not better either.

What justice, now that it's just us?

On the Bound

Wintertime when all things dead
Are frozen in the ground
The spring does fester
Beneath these things,
Life is on the bound.

The too-huge sky is grey and cloudy
The ground firm as ice.

Inside my heart beneath my skin
A thing is teeming a powerful heaving
Up through my throat and out of my mouth
Life and spring on the bound.

Jupiter in the Sky Above Seattle
(December 31, 2002)

As I look at the map, I now see
The magnitude of this move.
From sea to sea
The land could not be any greater
And the distance, equally so.
My you are far off.
Why not go to Jupiter or Pluto or Mars?
Creep away into night, loud as a rocket.
There's fire inside you, seething beneath your skin.

The Moon and Me

The moon convinced me that I can exist in the stratosphere/All I need is a means to get there/No spaceship no extra couple million dollars lying around to be the second woman/First black space tourist/Nah I can make it through by sheer will like the itty bitty gazillion pieces of space/Matter that hang in the sky/Eternity's disco balls/No scientist can convince me that she knows/How it all anchors itself/ Full to half to quarter to crescent

Material

I want to live a material life,
Not of material things,
But of material being.
There is nothing I need at the mall.

City Lights

City lights shining up the place
Neon signs bright on my face
I'm hanging around this town
Kicking rocks on the ground
Wondering where you got to
And my heart is blue but
What is a girl to do?

Broken Haiku

Hell bent like men living sin
You're not everything just most of it
Hell bent like men living sin

North Jersey Tracks

Pipes off roofs, truck yards, car dealers
Beat-down-grocery stores, barely selling food.
The snow takes up dust here.

Abandoned shells of industrial structures. Graffiti. Tire and axle
junkyard for clock-stamping wage workers. The ugliness outlay of
A powerful city.

Dumpsters, brick brown metal-sided high ceilings.
Busted out windows.
It's got to be a long way from here.

The backside of America, gated freight train
Graves, factory whistle land of
Lumberyards. Highway ramp
Exits winding Through domestic crumble
Exhaust pipe living.

Always steeples of churches. The sunset
Howling across the sky like the breath
Of a quittin' time whistle.

Used car lots, discount track beams.
6 am. Rust bridges, pothole roads.
More graffiti walls once-overed with paint.

It's got to be a very long way from here.

Red Brick City

Man in the alley
With a brown paper bag
Popping a can

A box of raisins and a tan straw hat

Man in the alley
Rest down easy

Peep the street
Behind the hedges
Tip one back
In the Red Brick City

Trail of the Southern Cross

Recant those tales you once told me.
With a little of the romance and of the
Women who slapped the faces of those who
Shouldn't touch.

Take me through the hot sands of Arkansas
That blue grass that grows straight round to Mississippi, Alabama-
Up the Delta.

When they went to punch cards in industry.
Chicago and Detroit.
And the ones that went
Straight up and clean
Through to Canada.

Did you know them? Are they kin? Of how they left to make a
place for us, but never came back.
We didn't know where to find them, but
Mostly, we didn't know where to look.

Make the sign of the southern cross.
Hoot if you're safe, bark if they're coming.

We'll find that crossroads
Where Little Robert Dusty became the man that
Sold his soul for the blues.
In the cemeteries where they are
Buried. In unmarked graves, we shall know them under foot.

Make the sign of the southern cross over
Hot sands and blue grass and factory smoke.

Mark the buildings that are ours,
Fair and square.

Where the river water flows

The rain has come and it wipes away the past so
Clean and the mud's a paste of what wasn't.

Seep back into the soil, deep back
Into the soil.
Where the dirt blows over itself,
Again and again.

People Taken & Displaced

Red for the blood of a million souls or more

People who could not, did not dream or
Hope under lock and key as
Entrails of a cargo ship

The fate of kings and queens,
High priestesses and warriors:
Chainedheadtonecktohandstofeet

Excrement and sickness
Packed together
One by one by one by one
Died like a dog and
Heaved to the undaunted sea.

White for the prickly bodies of a million cotton plants or more

People who could not, did not dream or
Hope under blistering sun, like pack mules,
They shuffled between the rows.

Blue is for the beautiful music that sprung into jazz

People who could not, did not dream or
Hope under star-lit skies as
A washtub drum and cardboard guitar
Plucked and pounded the doom
They could not speak.

The deaths of an enslaved people
The trace of their hard-knock lives
Slide deep into the flag waving on that mast.

For Maya & Langston

I know that caged bird like
The crusting over of a
Dream deferred.
One day the cage is empty
And the dream implodes.

II.

Truth

I will tell you something about
Time and space, It is all one in the same.

I move this way, you bend back like the night.
You move that way, I yearn for ya like the dawn.

I won't tell you the innermost of the outermost.
But I will give you what's within.
Posterity is ill-formed and misguided.

Give me truth and honesty in all the pain
It sometimes causes, and I'll heave back at you
The most beautiful thing that ever did live: reality.

It is your innermost that radiates the beautiful
Ugly truth. Your real thoughts illuminate your
Path. Will you worry or will you
Emanate the true beautiful glow inside of you?

Not at Home

I've called you friend
And fed you when
There wasn't enough to eat.

Even when your appetite
Was enough for both of us
You ate.

When my spirit was
Starving and I rang your bell,
You were not at home.

The Annals of Youth

The annals of youth are over
Locked away in a vault in the attic.

Innocence you must rely on
The kindness of some other stranger
From now on. You are someone else's
Problem. I am too world-weary to have
You near me. Be the glint in some other
Soul's eye for awhile.

For I have been befriended by
Wonderment who leads me
Bewildered to some other trough.

If We Be Bound

If we be friends then let it be so
If we be enemies then say it and go
If we be more then lay down your sword

Let us both be constant with this
Look into my eyes and tell me that

If we be bound then take my hand
If we be but souls passing then show dignity
If we be less then we shall never meet again

Look into my eyes and tell me this
And look into my heart and see that life

If we be lost–
If we be found–
If we be love –
Lay down your sword and
Let life bleed its course from the cuts.

Consumption

A heart so greedy
Another kissing helping
A first plate of a sumptuous feast
The last piece of meat carved out from my flesh

Slow Down Bunny

What I am is a slowly ticking
Fast paced hardly moving
Intrepidly seeking
Lethargically
Fleeting
Force

While time stands still around you
I race around the outside
You sit in a particular haze
The clock is ticking behind me

Destiny
Has moved
Chaotically we acquiesce
Like a leaf caught in a whirlwind,
A rock stuck and flung from the chariot wheel.

The Life of Air and Stone (For C.N.)

We come through a broken down life
That we can rebuild minute by minute.
Change comes so slowly, but somehow
Keeps things a-go.

Too bad time passes the way that it's gonna
'cause if I had eons I might change a little.

Instead it's only me
And my little thoughts
About great big things
That come into my head,
Treading a little, then out again.
Sometimes it's about you and me,
But mostly, of everything.

The pendulum swings far too wide
From side to side.

Time passes oh so slow between us
But after a while, things suddenly
Come into view.

We forget things, we live to forgive
(breathe fire)
We forgive things, we forget to live
(freezing life)
We live things, we forgive to forget
(throw stones)

The Innermost

We live silent lives
As though a mistake,
Some correction must be made.
Speak peacefully, do unto others.
Quietly I resurrect my lost self.
Missing something
Is vacant thought, where
Filling it is due.

Hot Coals

I am hobbled by your need
For me to burn and writhe
By your side.

I am humbled by your need
To breathe in my skin
Your yearning for my affection that –
Once you get, you let go, like I am
Hot coals burning your fingers.

We cement things with silence and looks.

Haiku

Be liquid hot gold
Flow and melt into something
Slink into crevices

Psalm for Mia

Higher than the moon
Wider than the sky
Just like the deepest ocean sea
It's bigger than me

Bleeding Against the Sky

What light are you sister,
What shade of ray from the galloping sun?

Are you now of the soft tangerine-creamed
Hues that creep from daybreak?

Or, are you more of a riotous ray, among those
Hard-charging chariot beams that burn the day
Through noon?

If I know you like I should, you are a seething
Kind of shade that swirls against the sunset,
Bleeding against the sky,
As though dying of blues and maroons.

Interlove

We see what has been conquered here
We see that we just might bake in this world
Under the sun with this crinkling skin and find
In each other, some of what we lack.

Time, distance, days only eat away from what
We thought we'd known of one another so long ago
On that first night, dripping with a
Longing/life/lust/love.

Hereafter, get what one can from this life.
One sees what one will have after this.

Something tough, something terminal.
Something soft at the core but everlasting.

Patterns

Sometimes the phone rang late at night
And the sun would be somewhere tired.

Simple things, simple plans
Needy things, needy hands.

Everything is mutable
Like my voice unlike my mind
racing.

Watch you walk into the night your
Coat clinging around the ears.

Bleeding from Our Fingers

We do these things
With our fingers
Cut and bleeding

We live this life
Like thorns in the
Rose oblivious to
The beauty they
Protect in the bloom

In the garden of the ages
We rake our own wounds
To fertilize what is yet to come

And therein the dust becomes our home

Les étapes de la vie

Stages and stages and stages
In the throes of the chaos
Time funnels strong winds
To separate the wheat from the chaff.

I hold hard to the wheel
As it turns and whips and whirls.
I hold tight with my arms and my legs
To the axis.

That which is not mine, I let go
Those things that remain cling to me
If you love something, let it go.

These are the stages of losing ground.

The stages of rebirth
Recognition
Resolution
Renewal.

These are the moments
That lead up to love's return.

Thrash

You're using my velocity like a terrible storm rakes in winds to
Feed its hungry eye; I lash out Wildly at the night amid palm trees.

Wreckage, damages lay in our wake as
We hash out and rehash what is done,
What will become.

Of course, the calm after, where we lay
Together in the night belies that there are
No answers to give.

Taking on Chance

Fate is a mean indulgent thing
Sending her daughter
Destiny to knock back a few
She plays her hand of trumps
King of Swords Queen of Cups
Man on a horse headed back to the fort
She laughs blithely at her all-knowing hand
While I got nothing but inferior suits

III.

A Little Knowledge

A little sunshine
Where I stand
To see which way to walk

A little silence
Before I sleep
To hear the planets talk

Some knowledge on a sunbeam
Divinity in a daydream
Is the only way I know I'm rowing
Down the right stream

We Here

Why are we here, but to question
Our earth
Our existence
Our reality

The ghosts are full here
Abound
Aplenty

Why are we here but to question
Our experience
Our past
Our remedies

Clicking Time

Here we are
Clicking time alongside
One another
Not knowing when
The clock will stop
For you or me.

Yet we plod on, we plod on.

Departures

Didn't want to face your leaving/for another Time and
space/Between the clouds/and the Ground/lifted up to a higher
Plane/standing on The edge/with my head in the ether/my
Feet planted on the ground/gonna follow that Wind/don't care
Where it bends/as long as I get There fast/spent my life
staring/Out of a Window/half my life/with nowhere to go

Things My Sister Thought

Running from the
Sown in seeds
You find they sprout up
At your feet

Take the time
To do things right
Today you retreat
Tomorrow you'll fight

You can not cheat
The truth is told
They may be things time forgot
But karma always knows

Taaffe

we'll stand in the places you stood
we'll drink at the places you drank
we'll swim where you swam
we'll run where you ran

we'll find pieces of you where you left them:

a hair in the shower
an unfinished work
a stack of magazines
a box of unread books
a couple of songs
a wide open grin

and we'll listen for your laughter on the wind.

We'll hike up a mountain and down again
we'll wear your clothes
we'll yell, JELLO BIAFRA! at the top of our lungs.
we'll smile at your favorite movies
we'll shed tears through our laughter

a life full of fire
a love undeniable
a friend unforgettable
a woman on the move

and we'll listen for your laughter on the wind.

Dear Lula

It seems that no one's old in Georgia anymore except fat ladies, like Miss Sweet Honey, with dark wet eyes. They sift black and white photographs, yellow and worn on the edges, of dead relatives. They've dropped off from too much Peach snuff, Bull of the Woods and spit cans. Too much Homemade Hooch and Sneaky Pete, too many hand-rolled Man-on-the-can's and, yes Lula, snipers who moonlight as lovers.

It seems that no one's got any memory in Cordele anymore, except for jilted men, whose women died long ago. And they finger keepsakes like faded hair ribbons and rusty barrettes, a Sunday dress and a hat or two. They spin embellished tales about how they treated their women, when they were alive, like Princesses and Queens. Even Granddaddy Pap. He sits on the porch, old as Methuselah now Lu, telling silent children in the backs of cars. Tells them, at your grave, in no uncertain terms, that he's prideless. *Her boyfriend shot her, dat how come yo grandmamma dead.* He even says I look like you around the eyes.

It seems that Big Mule didn't stop just because I lost something. People keep living and dying. Wet white paint dries quick in the heat on the concrete slap that seals you in the earth. And Lu, the sun don't set any quicker than it did before, now that you're gone. The snipers are gone and others took their place. Miss Sweet Honey sings a-cappella at funerals with loose teeth and dark gums, *Thank God I'm alive and not dead!* And Pap sits in the back quiet and crying.

Thank God I'm alive and not dead. Because the dead don't tell stories, they don't say how they died and the living forget the day you were born. Dear Lula, there's not much left around to say you were here except for what Pap says jumps out from around my eyes.

A Winter of Crows

Only the crows know
where the cold goes
in the bitterest of winters

It was you who said
When a murder flies
Across one's path,
A horrible omen
Is foretold.

I half-way believed, until
A winter of crows.

They gathered atop the trees
Outside of your window,
Plucking the truth from the bark
With their claws.

It was you who said
That when someone dies
In a room, you open their window
To free their soul.

I opened your window amid
A winter of crows.

You would know what it's like
To be free; and we would know
The price of that freedom.

www.ingramcontent.com/pod-product-compliance
Lightning Source LLC
LaVergne TN
LVHW050947080826
845145LV00004B/1443